<u>Acknowledgements</u>

I would like to thank everyone who
supported me through this journey;
through the tears, the smiles, the heartache,
and the redemption.
I love you all.

-cloudy <3

Captivation

-cloudy <3

Midnight suns-

Midnight suns
always made me smile.
happy moments in the dark do exist
like tripping over the rug
in front of the fireplace
and sleepovers in forts made
of pillows and love.
Nothing can hurt me
Everything in this moment
is possible.
Playful times I would never replace.

I'll never forget them
and with you by my side
I never thought I'd run out of
innocent memories to smile at

-cloudy <3

first love poem -

I know you don't hold your hands up for a God,

but I believe you were a blessing; a gift

and maybe it's a little too early for this

and my heart probably isn't equipped for love yet

but I love looking at you

every crease and crevice of you is fascinating

the way you play,

the way you customize ordinary and create

extraordinary

I saw you with eyes full of stars

and still kept you at a distance

sometimes I wish we were intertwined

holding you in my orbit

with gravity gluing us together

let's look up together

with you I can be sincere

on rolling hills devoted to me and you

-cloudy <3

we will always process things differently
yet we comprehend each others' story

surrounded by secrets and colors
both just quiet enough to listen to
our laughter after the downpour
teaching me how to be vulnerable
thank you for trying to understand me

I don't write love poems but I really, really like
you.

I want you to listen to why you're beautiful
when you hear the melody from a piano;
the birds filling the morning with joyous chirps,
and the overwhelming voices becoming softer
It's because you walked into the room

you've changed me and you might never know
I will always miss long hallways and hammocks
but when you get lonely

-cloudy <3

pick up the phone and tell me about your day

I still don't know how to write a love poem,
but I'm getting there
and it's all because of you.
I love you

-cloudy <3

The stacks-

we weren't the only ones,
there were thousands of couples
who had kissed before us
and thousands who would
kiss after us
but this one,
 the one that held the most meaning
it will echo through these books
and live in these poems
this kiss and this moment
will become a story passed down
through love and late night readings
it will calm storms
and it will be remembered

-cloudy <3

Endless-

with my tongue
tied to yours
I have forgotten
how to speak
and while trying to
come up with
the words to tell
you how beautiful
this is. I smile
because the rest of me
is too
lost in you to say how
much I never want this
to end

-cloudy <3

Remembering-

I don't understand you yet
but I plan to learn everything
you let me

I love how unpredictable
you are

but imagine me
knowing you on days you've
completely forgotten
yourself

-cloudy <3

Vulnerable-

"Now if I tell you I'm fine
Will you
Ignore everything
You've seen
Or
Make me tell
The truth" I said.
And you replied,
"That's a start"

-cloudy <3

O, how I love to love-

I love so hard sometimes,
I end up punching myself
in the gut

I love with such tenderness sometimes,
I get so soft that bruises and cuts appear
on my skin
I love so freely
I lose my filter
and allow everything in

I love like it won't kill me
And I love it.

-cloudy <3

The first time-

It was subtle, tender, and quite
it was resplendent

we moved together
with quiet whispers & loud love

we became one.

I always thought it'd be
 different.
I always thought it'd be
Someone else.
but by the grace of some god
It was you.

-cloudy <3

-

I want us to be invincible

i've been dismembered
I've been resilient
i've been unstable
and I've been brilliant

& I know were just human
flimsy, problematic, weird, stupid
human beings

but I don't want to be anything
without you.

-cloudy <3

-

What happened here was holy
I want to write stories
of us all over this city.

Nothing else seems more fitting for us
than nightlife
than Frankenstiens & mosaics
than coming alive in the dead of night
& becoming something oddly miraculous
becoming art
becoming whole again...

Just for a few hours

-cloudy <3

-

& all night we bonded with our bodies
 like the sun wouldn't come out tomorrow

As if time stopped in this room
And between us,
 it did.

-cloudy <3

And I get to wake up to such a humble beauty
I look at her & I think I want that
I want thousands of these moments
Every morning,
Every random cold sweat
Or when it's too hot
Or when there's not enough covers to get lost in
I want to wake up to you
& get lost in any and every way possible

-cloudy <3

-

she asked me if
i was addicted to him

i look at her and laugh.

"no one else can make me crave them as much as
he can",
i said between gasps of air and giggles;

in the end nothing was actually funny.

-cloudy <3

-cloudy <3

Quarrel

-

Unattainable
but necessary
like food for the soul

I don't know where I wandered too;

-cloudy <3

I miss home
I'm ravenous for comfort

but I have no key
and no map

I sit here stiff and aching
with no hands to hold and
no words or whispers saying
I miss you

Sitting-

Everynight I come back to the same
booth you left me in years ago
with my arms extended
and my placid palms open

-cloudy <3

I've been reaching out to you

I am waiting with an open mind
and forgiving heart

yes, of course, you've hurt me
but like my lungs need oxygen

I could never stop needing your love

so as the damaged person I am
I sit in this booth hoping,
that one day
you'll come
back to me

A Series of Drunk Poems-

The only thing in the universe
I love more than words

-cloudy <3

is you
forever & always

you.
`

I think I'd do anything to
be close to you,
to hold you in my mouth,
to have some type of ascendancy
over you

For so very long I wanted
to be raveled in your ethereal existence

& for so very long I was drained
of all my inclination
then I began to realize
you can only take what I make
available.
`

I dream of us

-cloudy <3

mainly you
& then there's me
dancing around the
idea of you dreaming of
me.
`

I will love words
even through they
don't love me
back
`

& all the things I imagined I'd do with you
that we never did
were things I could've done
alone all along
`

With all this time under our belt,
you'd think we'd figure out how to work.

by this time we're supposed
to be rid

-cloudy <3

of the kinks & technical difficulties

I thought we were done with
 the malfunctions & false starts

Just take my hand
you know me
you know us
we have lived us

The problem is we aren't
a perfectly oiled machine
our pieces don't match
& we won't work together
     -   Until we've grown
 `

When we love it's consuming.
Never ending

With my hand in yous
& your body in mine

-cloudy <3

Where else would I want to be

Pray for me,
for the good,
the bad
the ugly
& the beautiful
Pray that I make it to the
next poem
& pray that these words build homes
for those who can't find one
anywhere else

now I am the girl that
sits quietly & waits
I never wanted to be this version
of myself
    -   What happened to us
`Of all the words
That could be used

-cloudy <3

To describe us
& you choose
emotional
how shallow of you
`

There are small infinities
that hold our love
the place it still exists
that's where I live
between the lines
of then & now
`

One day
you left without
telling me you love me
& that was
the beginning
of the end.
`

I'm sorry that you found your name
in my rough drafts

-cloudy <3

I always change
It to a pronoun
before it prints
`

And I just needed karma
to not
come for me
just this once.
`

I can't keep writing poems about you
when I'm drunk
they come out slurred & blurred
& way too honest
all of my pain poured onto a page for people to see
my skin smells of sin & secrets seared by you
I wish we didn't want to be together
I wish I could wash you off of me
I hang onto your holiness in hope this will get
better

you and I have different end goals in mind

-cloudy <3

I am just a pit stop
while you, you were my destination
   -   Love on an open road; before the crash

-cloudy <3

Giving-

& after everything I'm still here
like shards of glass in skin
with blood, sweat, and guilt
I have been taken as a prisoner of war
no reparations for what has taken place here,
no angels to save me now

I have to want it.
I have to want to be, happy
I have to want to be alive ...
as if the tears weren't enough to
prove my love for you

you ask for more and I give,
without thought I give
instead of working on myself.

-cloudy <3

with every particle of my being you were loved
but you can't love back
and that's fine
Cause this heart is full of fireflies that want to
light the way

The amount of want I have for you is
immeasurable.

So I'll sit here as you chisel diminutive fragments
of me away,
until there's nothing left.

-cloudy <3

Scars-

I still can't remember myself
without these scratches;
without the black and blue,
without the scars you
gave me

and now I'm starting to scar myself

-cloudy <3

heartbreak is normal-

Heartbreak is normal;
Heartbreak is waking up
without you. It is
unconditional love being taken
and returned with conditions.

It is thousands of dead humming
birds in the pit of my stomach

Heartbreak is diminished hope.
It is every precious thing
becoming mundane

Heartbreak is trying to move forward

-cloudy <3

but standing in place

It is loving recklessly with no regrets,
expectations, or expiration dates
Heartbreak is wondering why, you
woke up with a beating heart
 when you don't have theirs.

It is breathing water
Heartbreak is never getting out what you gave in,

Heartbreak is normal

-cloudy <3

The cost of loving you-

The cost of convincing you to love me
is too high a price
i can give you all of me
and the efforts wouldn't be enough

after loving you for the third time
i started to name my bruises
by which girl you chose
Apparently they were just expensive
enough for you to love them back

-cloudy <3

-cloudy <3

When love runs out-

When the love is no longer enough what do we
do?

Do we fight
Do we leave
Do we cry

and how am I supposed to move on when
everywhere and everything
reminds me of you...

-cloudy <3

you said i hurt you
 "deeply"
you said you loved me
"deeply"

i responded,
 i wish you weren't lying

-cloudy <3

Little nothings-

and just like that
when i had thought
all hope was lost...
there you were on a rainy day
holding everything i wanted to hear
and you recited it
Perfectly

-cloudy <3

Honesty-

i lied the last time i said i love you
and I didn't mean to

I had said it so many times before
I guess the meaning just faded away

i'm sorry-- I didn't mean to
but i did

we've been what they call sitting ducks
drifting in opposite directions
without a rope to bring us back to each other

it's time to let go now

-cloudy <3

Losing myself-

i don't know what else
i can give
i hate you
as much as
i love you
and i can't keep playing
a game that isn't meant
for me,
especially when you
Always win in the end

-cloudy <3

Space-

There's always been
An infinity
Of space
 Between us
So much dark
space, even on those
Nights with
You in
Between
My arms
I can still see
Galaxies in your eyes

-cloudy <3

Nothing-

Speechless
and absolutely
powerless.
there is nothing
I can do to bring
you back to me
I wonder when
forever ended
for you

-cloudy <3

Small tears
for big fears

I can feel them in my stomach,
in my chest.
On my heart

blood boiling and
Faith coaling

only you can fix this.
do you want to fix me?
~broken things

-cloudy <3

-cloudy <3

Ode to you-

When I finally get over you,
 There are so many things I will be able to do
without crying
Like listening to slow songs
Or sitting in a mom van
Or fake arguing in public to make others
uncomfortable
Like not flinching after I make a smart remark

I will be able to throw out the hoodie I told you I
lost

-cloudy <3

I will be able to listen to my favorite music
I will be able to go to the ice cream shop
and not wonder what it'd be like
if we ever went on an actual date

I still wish we went on an actual

I will be able to talk to my friends that always
accidently bring you up
It's been so long since I've laughed with them;
And maybe I'll make amends with the friends I
lost over you
I still don't know if you were worth them

I will try to stop comparing people who show
interest in me, to you
Not everyone is superman or woman

When I can finally go to a basketball game
without hating myself

-cloudy <3

reminded of how I let you pick me up and throw
me back down
Dribbling my emotions, when it was most
convenient for you
And how you treated us like a game.
I know you loved the game,
I'm still unsure about your feelings towards me

I will stop bringing you up when my sister talks
about love
And when my mom asks me
how you're doing I won't become glass,
because I can't answer
Or because you are doing fine without me.

You tear me apart just by smiling in my direction
And sometimes you don't mean to,

It's just that after I would pour out my heart,
you'd laugh
And that damn smile haunted me until

-cloudy <3

I hated smiling myself
but when i'm finally over you
I will be able to see you
and my heart won't become
the world's worst escape artist
beating on the inside of my chest looking for
asylum

I will be able to breathe
Inhale someone new and push you out
My system won't need you anymore
I will listen when you show me who you are
And learn to love myself

When I am finally over you
You will merely be a figment but not of my
imagination
A monster that is no longer in the dark

When I am finally over you

-cloudy <3

I will whisk the memory of you away
Just enough to remember who I am.

Odds & Ends

-cloudy <3

Pieces-

Holding your pretty
Heart in pieces
You come to me
(A stream stress)
Wanting me to sew you
Back together

But darling

-cloudy <3

all I have left are
Thimbles too thin to
Protect me,
Needles that have been
Splitting at its ends.

You have asked too much of me:
And I haven't asked enough of you

-

letting you be happy is the closest
I'll ever get be to being happy
because if I can't do it
I want someone else to;
I think we all deserve that
I just have to wait and hope
　　　　~wishing the best for you

-cloudy <3

-

I've been walking
through the forest
looking for a map
Hoping when I find it,
it'll bring me to
something,
anything,
that'll breathe

-cloudy <3

me back to
life

~oxygen thief

-

i miss you
on the days
i'm scattered like
the stars.

but tonight i'm a meteor;
whole and illuminating

-cloudy <3

millions of light years
away from you
& still important

I have all this fire
in me.
it'd be a shame
if you got burned.

Sorryy-

Today you came to me naked
then I stripped you of some more skin

I had some holes to fill

I'm sorry you became just another body,
it wasn't supposed to happen that way.

-cloudy <3

-

I started to get rid of you
The way I shed hair
slowly and without recognition.
every morning I get up
And brushed more of you out of me
                    ~simply done

-cloudy <3

Moving on-

When I look at you I see beauty.
I see time;
I see value,
I see journey
I see fight
I see punch; I feel punch
in chest, in heart

-cloudy <3

so much pain.

So I punch back
and say I can do whatever I want

Today I am fight
Today I am power
and tomorrow I will try, to be as strong
as I was today
and from now on

I am freedom.

-

& on days like today
pick yourself up

dust off yesterday
and get ready
for today. you are

-cloudy <3

Brilliant,

undeniably brilliant.
Act like it
        ~you already knew this

-

My vagina is not a vacation
from your girlfriend's body

to you I am just
perishable anatomy
but I am someone else's
home

-cloudy <3

~we are not in love, just lonely

-

I started to get over you
the way I shed hair
slowly & without recognition

every morning I get up
& brush more of you off of me
              ~piece by piece

-cloudy <3

-

No one thinks it'll end when it does
some can breathe through it
some can work through it
some can fight through it
but I have been fighting for
too long

-cloudy <3

I have stepped in rings
with my fists up and feet planted
and I've been hit with things
indigestible

when every ounce of you is gone
and there is no more fight in you

it's ok you can let go.

-

He hates when
I make myself
hornier than he can
but I got tired
 of censoring
my sexual tendencies
for his comfort

-cloudy <3

It takes time-

my friends tell me it'll take time
but it's gonna be okay

i dont have anymore pieces to give

-cloudy <3

everytime i see you
i watch a decade go by

i can't be with you
or touch you
but my mind won't let me forget your smell,
your smile,
your corny jokes,
your scars.

i love you and a part of me will always be rooted
in you

how do i get rid of you
when the most precious parts of me have you
embedded in them

I'll have you out of me one day,
i just hope i remember who i am after the
surgery.

-cloudy <3

Closure-

I hope my
Inevitable death
Will give you
Something
That I couldn't
Something

-cloudy <3

A little like
Closure.

-

how dare you suggest
that my love isn't stable enough
for the both of us

-cloudy <3

& how dare you convince yourself
my affection for you isn't authentic.

who do you think you are,
to invalidate the way I feel
towards you?

I spent years trying to assure that I am
permanently here
and unconditionally accepting who you are

so I call bullshit.
it's not me who can't love
it's you;
it has always been you

-

I suppose the only word that
could capture sorrow
is goodbye

-cloudy <3

good bye to who I was
good bye to those I loved
and good bye to who I never got to be

good bye never
 gave anyone placidity
but maybe I'm different

so goodbye to you
let's hope that something
exceptional happens

-cloudy <3

Reflection

-cloudy <3

No one thinks it'll end when it does

Some can breathe through it,
Some can work through it,
Some can fight through it;
But I have been fighting for
too long

I have stepped in rings
& been hit with things
Objectionable.
When every ounce of you is gone
& there is no more fight in you

It's ok,
You can let go

-cloudy <3

An ode to my one night stands lover-

Dear stranger,

i found it only fitting that i share something
intimate with you

i've had sex with people i had no business sleeping
with
i've wrapped myself in another woman's hard
work
and indulged in another man's blessing

and i take them like free samples at a grocery
store
bump into them
as if at a party with too many people
and too little light

some call me reckless,

-cloudy <3

inconsiderate

but remember you have been in the equation
longer than i have.
we have never been in direct contact
there might be traces of you
but i am not playing detective
you are a coefficient, the number that doesn't
change
and i;
i am a variable.

plug me or another girl in and that determines
the product

see i can be replaced
today i feel replaceable
like there is and
has never been
any significance to my existence

-cloudy <3

it's a cold morning
but my cheeks are filled with fire
and the only thing keeping
the smoke at bay are my eyelids
my whole body feels heavy
and out of place,
like God trying to
tell me to shrink
and I guess I agree;
because I'm curled up
in a corner trying to be
invisible.
and it's been like this most of my life
as a kid I curled up in the classroom during
recess
and at home I curled up under covers
Then I found myself in dim lit coffee shops
and behind the rest of the crowd
hoping to never be seen
and only heard when absolutely necessary

-cloudy <3

I think I have a bad habit
of giving my body as a souvenir
to the people who find me.
The people who hear me
when I least expect it,
and tell me
I might be hard to find but they do see me

just for them to disappear
the next morning
and I guess
I'm the maker of my mess
I am a horribly crafted person
who is being kept together
by tape and glue
but I am carrying burdens made of boulders

and I can only blame myself
so I asked questions like
what if this universe isn't real

-cloudy <3

and what if this never happened
and what if you aren't hurt

because i can apologize
 for the thoughtless night
I spent with your future

or i can explain why this is not my story
it is yours
what we made was regrettable
but it *is* in the past

it only lives on
in those little infinities
 no one bothers to look at any more

i am hoping this isn't too confusing for you.

Signed; i'm not sorry but my deepest
condolences—

-cloudy <3

i hope this wasn't too much honesty for you to
handle

goodbye stranger

-

when i've given you everything
& put in the work to be better

the scares don't just go away
they'd fade slowly.
but underneath the paint;
if you peel it back

there are ocean deep wounds
covered in weak bandaids
made of leftover love
& forgotten fortitude

-cloudy <3

Do not act as if you were perfect
& Do not act as if I am wrong
when I am resilient

Awkward Encounters-

You told me you don't want to be
One of my poems
You said you didn't want this to be weird
& it wasn't
Until you said something.

We could have left everything up in the air
And shared nothing,
But that night
& those words
But now this is **weird**.
it is closed off interactions

-cloudy <3

& taking breathing breaks in the bathroom.

I left without your number for a reason
We were just a night
A moment
A blimp in time

& it might have been beautiful
But it was never supposed to be forever

There is nothing wrong with heated hookups
It's the awkward encounters
That are never acceptable

-cloudy <3

Stains-

Today I am wearing polka dots
& watching you with another lover

They're probably wearing lace
& overpriced perfume
And you're learning how to map out their
anatomy

but I'm in your muscle memory
We have years of tracing each other
Behind us

-cloudy <3

And i'm not sad
im not angry
You have been walking forward
& so have I

But there times when I look at their body
And sometimes,
When they're mapping out mine
I find myself getting
Knocked into nostalgia
& reaching for your reflection

You may not understand
but I miss you just enough
to remember your body,
But not enough to want
You under mine again

Like a faded stain
You are here
But you are not needed

-cloudy <3

Digestible-

there is a folklore that if you swallow a piece of
gum
it takes your body seven years to completely digest
it

I was five the first time I heard that it took
seven whole years to digest one piece of
bubblegum
as any curious and right minded five-year-old
would do

-cloudy <3

I asked my grandma to buy me a pack of gum
and after I chewed and swallowed a whole pack
of spearmint 5 gum
I was so proud of myself
I had a smile that stretched from ear to ear
that proved that I had just accomplish
something incredible
in seven years I would free this gum for my body
and it would be lime green and minty
and there is nothing better than that to a five
year old

when I was 12 I find out that the body never
fully digest corn
as any intelligent 12 year old would do
I fell in love with corn and ate it every night
with dinner
I figured this way I could never die of starvation
my body had enough energy to live off of
plus corn was healthy and yellow

-cloudy <3

and for a self-conscious 12-year-old there's
nothing better than bright and healthy

I was 14 when I met you

I was 15 when I learned that you weren't
something I could digest and just let go in a few
years
you weren't something that would get lost in my
digestive tract
you held on to all the nitty gritty crevices of me
you were hard to scrape out
you found your way to my heart

as any 14-year-old girl would do I approached
and ingested you with no caution
I walked into you with open palms
a ready heart
and a naive mind
and there were dozens of signs
they all pointed me elsewhere

-cloudy <3

warned of danger
and tried to build a wall between us

but you made me laugh
And when you smiled it was like nothing else
mattered
you were the beginning middle and end to a story
you were the sun
the moon
the stars
the tide
gravity

you were like a piece of home
you were the window
the door
the roof
you were the whole damn room
you made my digestive tract your bitch
no toxins could touch you
i never stood a chance

-cloudy <3

and enliven though i tried to come out the other
end with minimal damage
i choked on reality when you got done me

i figured that if i'd take you in smaller portions
i would be able to keep my body at bay
if i could love like atoms bond
unrecognized and undetected

that maybe it'd all be ok

but when i began to regurgitate
pieces of myself trying to
to take you on

i realized that some things just aren't meant to
be inside of me
some things are simply indigestible

-cloudy <3

Such Luck -

He said he loved me
& I ask what exactly he meant
he started with how he loved

-cloudy <3

my mouth
said its overindulgent and profundity
was more comfortable than others

said that for right now I was
what he wanted,
what he liked;
but never forgot to remind me
I was disposable
only useful for the moment

temporary warmth & worship

At first this honesty hurt
but because these
fleeting feelings
showed me all I didn't want

there was relief in your evil,
liberation in your licentious,
& calamity in the midst of catastrophe

-cloudy <3

wow,

How lucky am I, to not love you anymore

What I Know Of Love -

all of my friends are falling in love
& I don't know who would

-cloudy <3

do that to themselves —subjected
to a relationship—

it took me a while
but, I am dating
or as my friends call it
practice for falling in love.
I've heard the horror stories
& warnings

so i can write about love all day
i can write about the ups
the downs
the do's
the don'ts
and the aftermath

But believe me
it'd all sound like madness
& it is

-cloudy <3

Love is magic, madness, and everything but
mediocre
Love is all you have stored in your pantry
being dumped into one pot
it is sorcery and sanctity

it is giving yourself over to someone else,
a journey over mountains and a walk over mounds

Love is confusion,
it is a chemical imbalance in your brain
Love is a drug
people search for it like dophines
looking for a dealer
and some can't handle reality
without a hit

intimacy is nothing to play around with
I always warn kids to stay away from that thing
they call love
because it is MADDENING

-cloudy <3

it is every emotion in one word
it is you had me at "hi"
and poems in the rain

it is let this stranger in
and completely hijack your life
and feel incomplete without them

it is 20 years together without any regrets
it is give them your best and worst
love is pretending to like their taste in music
and their unusual habits

Love is an everyday decision to not give up on this
person
to have committed to the institution that is them
it is a promise to try
to be their better half

people fall in love
hoping that it's dipped in forever.

-cloudy <3

forgetting that it's work
tears
effort
trial & error
it's learning how
to be lenient and understanding

love is invisible
so you'll need to keep a collection
of faith and patience
in your back pocket at all times
you'll have to learn spells
and how to formulate potions of all kinds
seek asylum in your lover
and recognize that there is such a wide array of
flaws
presented by different souls
and just like yours,
your lover has beautiful and boundless
blemishes
so if all the things

-cloudy <3

i could tell you about live
i choose to say that love
is invincible,
unprecedented,
and unique to everyone's chemical imbalance.

love is magic, madness, and everything but
mediocre

-cloudy <3

The social experiment -

Who are you to tell me I'm not warm enough for
summertime
I know that I can decide myself
But you don't know me like the sun
You've never seen my horizon

To the people who tell me my body is a temple
I've know what you're saying for years
It was taught to me by churches
Relatives
And mentors
It's been said in so many scenarios
its lost all meaning to me
I don't find intimacy, intimate
When I invite someone into my temple
it is for temporary prayers and penetration
I don't want worship

-cloudy <3

I want wonders to be uncovered
This is a classroom
And today is show and tell
Teach me something new
And I will touch you so tender
You'll want to tether me to testimonies and
Keep me under you forever
But I am not looking for love here .
I'm looking for laughable moments and
Lounging around in lingerie
I'm looking for momentary magic in meaningless
movements
Because baby, I still have healing to do
My body has never felt like a temple
No holiness, just wholes
No commitments, just cautions
There's been yellow tape around this
crime scene for as long as I can remember
For as long as i can remember
Dead bonds and bodies are tallying up inside me
And until tonight we were far from familiar

-cloudy <3

I am no princess
I am not delicate
This body is not a temple
It's a vessel
And I choose
Who can occupy it
When they occupy it
And how

If there were a God here,
It'd be me
I'm trying to figure out how these people think
they
Know about my body my body than I do
Honey, you will never understand
How this vessel effects my mind
Or how it feels when the prayers were over
This body only has its self
It needs no guidance.
you telling me my body is

-cloudy <3

A temple, is like a white man
Explaining racism to a women of color

You know nothing of this physique.
What its endured and learned.
There are lessons all over it that
Only I can decipher.
All this time I've been creating a masterpiece

Ive been gaining what I need
Without explanation
Without regret
Without shame
I have occupied this vessel
And became the only provider
My body has traveled between the
Layers and levels in its lovers
What I'm trying to say is
You can not tell me what this body is
You cannot love it better than I can.
So when you feel like telling my body is a temple

-cloudy <3

Please stop.

Before I was ever told about worship
I fell in love with deception and desperation
 And now I have to pay for it.
I have to get up and amend all the wrong I did
in the aftermath, I had to grow
This body is rediscovering how to love itself
Before loving anything foriegn
So please stop preaching to me what I do not
listen to
This is the path taken by the brave ones
I let myself be deferential to worthless words and
Faint fantasies
Forgive me if I don't listen anymore
But I can't give anymore pieces for anyone's
opinion
I am sunday candy

Who are you to tell me I'm not warm enough for
summertime

-cloudy <3

I know that I can decide for myself
But you don't know me like the sun
You've never seen my horizon

Finale-
This is redemption
Understanding,
Closure,
Etc.

This has taught me everything
about how to not love
but how to cherish,
                    flourish,
be comfortable

For us it was over a long time ago

-cloudy <3

For me it's just finishing
The lights went down

This whole performance lasted
longer than it should've anyways
I fell into painful pleasure
There was satisfaction in this
bondage to you
but this is rebirth,
Freedom,
Etc.

This is me
Not us.
No more lights,
Cameras, curtains
Or crowds
I don't want to be an extra in anyone
Else's movie

I am light

-cloudy <3

I am lesson
I am divine
I am living with legends to tell
I have a story,
not a script
there are no more
 fingers to point
or encores
we played tap dance
tug-o-war for too long
Trust me, none of you
 could fathom this story
If you tried

All the behind the scenes work:
The special effect emotions
then designing desires
with lying lights

I'm so ready to be myself
with no attachments

-cloudy <3

correlations

or associations

take a final bow

say goodbye

realize that the world has so much to

offer me

and you

outside of this theater

so let's explore without;

without a glance backwards.

-cloudy <3